Your Future as a
TEACHER

HIGH-DEMAND CAREERS™

Your Future as a
TEACHER

RACHEL GIVEN-WILSON AND ANNALISE SILIVANCH

Published in 2020 by The Rosen Publishing Group, Inc.
29 East 21st Street, New York, NY 10010

Copyright © 2020 by The Rosen Publishing Group, Inc.

First Edition

All rights reserved. No part of this book may be reproduced in any form without permission in writing from the publisher, except by a reviewer.

Library of Congress Cataloging-in-Publication Data

Names: Given-Wilson, Rachel, author. | Silivanch, Annalise, author.
Title: Your future as a teacher / Rachel Given-Wilson and Annalise Silivanch. Description: First edition. | New York : Rosen YA, 2020. | Series: High-demand careers | Includes bibliographical references and index. | Audience: Grades: 7–12.
Identifiers: LCCN 2018052987| ISBN 9781508187950 (library bound) | ISBN 9781508187943 (pbk.)
Subjects: LCSH: Teaching—Vocational guidance—Juvenile literature. | Teachers—Juvenile literature.
Classification: LCC LB1775 .G58 2020 | DDC 371.10023—dc23 LC record available at https://lccn.loc.gov/2018052987

Manufactured in China

Contents

Introduction 6

Chapter 1
WHAT DOES IT TAKE TO BE A TEACHER? 9

Chapter 2
EARLY EDUCATION AND ELEMENTARY SCHOOL TEACHERS 20

Chapter 3
MIDDLE SCHOOL AND HIGH SCHOOL TEACHERS 33

Chapter 4
GETTING YOUR FIRST TEACHING JOB 45

Chapter 5
THE FUTURE OF TEACHING 56

GLOSSARY 67
FOR MORE INFORMATION 69
FOR FURTHER READING 73
BIBLIOGRAPHY 74
INDEX 77

Introduction

There's a well-known saying that everyone remembers his or her favorite teacher. Teaching is a lot of work, but it's a great career for people who really want to make a difference. Teachers may teach in preschools, elementary schools, middle schools, or high schools. They may work in public schools, private schools, or charter schools. Most elementary school teachers work with a specific grade level, while middle and high school teachers choose a subject to teach and work with students in a range of grades.

INTRODUCTION

The most successful teachers are those who can make the subject matter engaging for their students. When kids are having fun, they are more likely to learn and retain information.

If you think you might be interested in becoming a teacher, it's a good idea to think carefully about what the job really involves and to make sure you have the right personality to be a teacher. When teachers genuinely enjoy and connect with their work, they can help to motivate an entire class full of students, as well as having a positive impact on their fellow teachers and school administrators.

"Great teachers recognize that what they do is simply who they are," says retired teacher Jeaninne Escallier

Your Future as a TEACHER

Kato, quoted in a 2015 article on Rasmussen College's website. "They understand that teaching is an extension of who they were meant to be."

Teaching is about much more than just educating students. It's about forming connections with each and every student in the class and supporting all of them in a whole range of ways. Rebecah Freeling, an early childhood education director quoted in the same article, says:

> I love teaching because teaching allows me to give a child the experience of someone who really gets them and accepts them for who they are, without making them bad or wrong. So often kids don't have that person in their life, especially if they're problem kids. And I feel that it's an honor to be that person.

Teaching is a stable career because teachers are always needed, whatever the economy is like. Aspiring teachers should note that there is more demand for certain kinds of teachers, such as special education teachers, and for teachers who are willing to work in high-need schools in urban or rural communities. If you're a hard worker who is willing to be flexible about where you work, you stand a good chance of being hired as a teacher.

Teaching isn't for everybody, but if you're a compassionate and generous person who loves working with children, you may just have what it takes to transfer your passion into a meaningful career as a teacher. "I truly believe that teaching is the most important profession in modern society," says Kato. "Other than doctors, teachers hold human lives in their hands each and every day."

Chapter 1

WHAT DOES IT TAKE TO BE A TEACHER?

Teachers choose to teach because they love learning and helping children or teens to learn, too. Most teachers choose a grade level or area to specialize in. Teachers are creative people who enjoy finding ways to present information to children in new and exciting ways. They do more than simply present information. Teachers must be able to think on their feet, reacting to and working with the students in the room.

OPTIONS IN TEACHING

Teachers have different job descriptions, depending on the grade level they teach. In early education environments, teachers act more as guides while children adjust to the social rules of school. Elementary teachers help students develop basic skills in reading, writing, and mathematics. In middle school, teachers help students focus on learning

Your Future as a TEACHER

while peer pressure rises around them. In high school, students are starting to discover and develop their talents, and an encouraging teacher can help them do this. Teachers' own education, experiences, and personality may help define what age group and subject matter they prefer to teach.

Public school teachers cannot teach without a valid teaching certificate, or license, in their state. This license specifies what grades one is qualified to teach. For example, a teaching certificate might state that a person

If you're considering a career as a teacher, give some thought to the kind of school you'd like to work at. Teaching varies a lot from one school to another.

WHAT DOES IT TAKE TO BE A TEACHER?

is qualified to teach elementary grades one through six. Teachers in grades seven through twelve need a certificate in secondary education, with an endorsement, or approval, in their subject area. Teaching music requires its own certificate, but this certificate typically can include all grades, kindergarten through grade twelve. Private school teachers can often teach without certification if they have a bachelor's degree.

IMPORTANT TEACHING SKILLS

While being a "people" person is helpful, a teacher in training also develops and practices the specific teaching skills needed in the classroom. An effective teacher must plan a course of study appropriate to an age group and then manage the class's attention and interest. A teacher evaluates each student's understanding of concepts and his or her social and emotional functioning in the classroom. Finally, a teacher needs to get along with and share ideas with other teachers, as well as communicate with parents and welcome their questions. Over time, teachers learn the best ways to approach the challenges in each area.

PREPARING FOR TEACHER CERTIFICATION

To get a teaching license, it is necessary to complete courses in teaching and in content areas (arts and sciences). Each state's education department specifies which courses it requires for each certificate. Teacher trainees also need to practice teaching in a classroom, with

Your Future as a **TEACHER**

supervision, for a certain number of hours. Finally, most states require teachers to pass one or more certification tests before they can get a license. These standardized tests require teachers to show they meet basic standards in reading, writing, math, and other subjects. The exams also test knowledge of the craft of teaching.

All states require teachers to have at least a bachelor's degree. Some aspiring teachers get a bachelor's degree in teacher education, while others pursue teacher education as part of a master's degree program after college. For early education and elementary school,

Training for elementary school teachers focuses on core subjects, such as English and math, and on the ways in which kids learn.

WHAT DOES IT TAKE TO BE A TEACHER?

a teacher education program includes courses in specific subjects, such as math and English, and on teaching and learning itself. To prepare students for middle and high school certification, programs focus heavily on the subject the individual wants to teach.

As part of most programs, students need to do one or two student-teaching internships. As a student teacher, one assists in a real classroom and learns from a head teacher. A teacher education program usually places students in a classroom near the college campus. Each program has a list of cooperating teachers who have agreed (and may be trained) to work with students from the college. Some colleges allow students to complete student teaching while working at a first job in a school (as an assistant teacher, for example). Students who do this can earn money while completing their requirements. Some programs even allow students to do their student teaching in a foreign country.

Student teachers are asked to demonstrate the social skills that make a good teacher. They should be able to get students to trust them and motivate them to do good work. They should show that they are aware of, and sensitive to, students' academic and cultural differences and treat each student with respect. After spending time observing their cooperating teachers, student teachers have the chance to plan and carry out their own lessons with students.

Wherever one enrolls in a teacher education program, it is important to be sure that the program is an officially approved one. The Council for Accreditation of Educator Preparation (CAEP) has a list of approved programs.

Your Future as a **TEACHER**

What Makes a Great Teacher?

A teacher with passion and creativity makes the classroom come alive with ideas, discussion, and engaging activities. The qualities of patience and cooperation create a peaceful place for learning, free of conflict. Energy and enthusiasm are also important. A teacher needs to find a way to motivate students who may be tired, distracted, or discouraged. Organization is key for planning lessons and grading papers.

Different grade levels require different skills and personalities when it comes to teaching. Preschool teachers should be caring so that their young students feel safe.

WHAT DOES IT TAKE TO BE A TEACHER?

Finally, teachers may need authority most of all because if students don't respect a teacher's guidelines, no learning can take place.

Different grade levels require different personalities, or at least an ability to change one's approach. Preschool and kindergarten students feel safe in an unfamiliar environment if their teacher is understanding and caring. Fifth graders appreciate a little wackiness from a creative teacher since they are beginning to plug into their own talents and confidence. Middle and high school students will admire a teacher who leads the class with respectful authority, but also brings humor into the classroom.

APPLYING FOR TEACHER CERTIFICATION

After completing the requirements for a teaching license, it is necessary to apply to the state department of education. This involves filling out forms, supplying proof that you have completed all of the requirements, and paying application fees.

Aspiring teachers should make sure that the teaching program in which they are planning to enroll leads to certification in the state of their choice. Students can be more confident that they will take all the courses needed for certification if they enroll in a state-approved program. Also, students should be sure they will receive a license for the exact class they want to teach, whether it is a grade level or a special subject.

Many states give all new teachers a provisional license. Teachers with this license must work in the classroom for a few years before receiving a permanent license. Even a permanent teaching license usually does not last the length of a teaching career. Most states require teachers to earn additional credits in order to renew their licenses every few years. Some states require high school teachers to earn a master's degree within a few years of becoming a teacher.

A NATIONAL LICENSE TO TEACH

Some experienced teachers who show additional teaching skill can apply for a national teaching license through the National Board for Professional Teaching Standards (NBPTS). This certificate is not required to teach in any state. However, it allows teachers the option to teach in another state without going through an entire state certification process.

After working as a teacher for some time, a teacher can apply for this license by collecting a portfolio of classroom work and taking a written test of teaching knowledge. By earning a national license, a teacher may be eligible for a higher salary. Individuals may also be able to get the certificate costs repaid. For more information on this license, contact the National Board for Professional Teaching Standards.

ALTERNATE ROUTES

Most states offer other ways to become a teacher, especially for those who are willing to teach in a geographic area or subject that has a teacher shortage. These alternate route programs allow people with college degrees in fields other

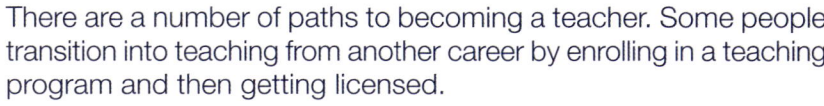

There are a number of paths to becoming a teacher. Some people transition into teaching from another career by enrolling in a teaching program and then getting licensed.

than education to become certified teachers. Each state offers its own guidelines on how to complete this training.

Those taking an alternate route may begin teaching under a head teacher while they take education courses on the side. Some alternate programs approve people to teach for one or two years before they receive permanent licenses. States that desperately need teachers may give out emergency licenses, which allow people to start teaching right away.

The alternate route is helpful for people who are older and may be working in another career but then decide that they want to become a teacher. Individuals who want to teach math and science may find more of these programs since there is a greater need for these teachers. Also, urban schools that have a shortage of teachers may offer programs like this. Vocational education teachers may enjoy an alternate route to teaching without a college degree if they can demonstrate talent in their field. Those who are interested in taking the alternate route can contact school districts or state departments of education for more information.

A STABLE PROFESSION

Teaching is generally a stable job. While schools are not immune from economic downturns, public schools with many students do not close overnight. Public schools are supported by taxpayer dollars. If a town's school board decides to make big changes to the school budget, taxpayers usually have the opportunity to approve it or reject it, and teachers usually get plenty of notice about such changes. Moreover, public schools guarantee a level of security for teachers and administrators who have shown themselves to be capable. After several years of working successfully in a school district, you can be eligible for tenure, which comes with protection from suddenly being fired. Private schools and charter schools are subject to different rules and may offer less job security.

About half of all teachers in the United States belong to a union. A union is a work association that bargains for a salary and benefits for its members. Unions also bargain for limits to work hours and days and push for

WHAT DOES IT TAKE TO BE A TEACHER?

better working conditions in schools. Preschool teachers and private school teachers are less likely to belong to a union than public school teachers.

Looking ahead, more jobs are expected for new teachers as the overall population continues to grow and as schools continue to set new goals for academic achievement. Also, many experienced teachers are expected to retire and new teachers will be needed to replace them. In 2018, the Bureau of Labor Statistics projected that jobs for kindergarten and elementary school teachers would grow by 7 percent and jobs for middle and high school teachers would grow by 8 percent. These growth rates are about as fast as the average for most occupations. It is important to note that there are generally more jobs for teachers in urban and rural areas, rather than suburban areas.

Chapter 2

EARLY EDUCATION AND ELEMENTARY SCHOOL TEACHERS

Prospective teachers should consider which ages of children they are interested in working with. The duties of a kindergarten teacher are obviously very different from those of a ninth-grade teacher. People who enjoy working with young children may decide to focus on learning to become an early education or elementary school teacher.

EARLY EDUCATION AND ELEMENTARY SCHOOL TEACHERS

EARLY EDUCATION

Teachers who work with the youngest students (preschool and kindergarten) typically have their own classrooms and work with the same group of students for the entire year. Early education teachers work hard to design their classrooms with young students in mind. The classroom will usually have areas for different activities: a play area, a quiet reading area, a "circle" area (where students can

Preschool classrooms are often divided into areas for different activities, such as reading, playing, circle time, and arts and crafts. Children spend short periods of time in each area.

Your Future as a TEACHER

sit as a group for a lesson or song), and an area of desks or tables for academic work or art.

At the preschool level, a typical day is structured in small sections of time (sometimes only fifteen minutes) with activities that change often. Education at this level is more social than academic: students practice taking turns, raising their hands to speak, and working together. Students also work on skills in preparation for elementary academics. For example, children develop motor skills through painting or sand play. Early language skills are taught through stories, games, and songs. Introductory math and science skills are involved in counting, building, and nature exploration. Dance, music, and all kinds of art are often used to stimulate young learners.

In the past, kindergarten classes were play-based, half-day programs that were similar to preschool. However, that is no longer the case in many areas. Concerns about children's academic readiness and the need for parents to work have caused schools to develop more academic, full-day programs. Most school districts house kindergarten programs within their elementary schools. Kindergarten teachers now instruct children in phonics (connecting letters to sounds) and early math (recognizing patterns, counting, and doing simple addition). The kindergarten curriculum also includes music, social studies, science, and sometimes even computers. In a full-day kindergarten classroom, teachers plan a day that allows for the natural rhythms of snacks, lunch, and rest time along with lessons and activities.

More children than ever are enrolled in early education programs. Some regions have even introduced public pre-kindergarten programs, which provide public education for children starting at the age of four. New York City has universal pre-K, meaning every child in the city can enroll in a publicly funded pre-K program at the age of four. Early childhood education programs are likely to continue to grow as long as local and state education boards can fund them.

ELEMENTARY SCHOOL

After the shift to academic work in kindergarten, the elementary school teacher's instructional role in the classroom expands. Actual teaching time increases as children's attention spans do, and the subject matter becomes more complex.

Most classroom teachers in first through sixth grade teach a number of basic academic subjects—including math, reading, writing, and social studies—to the same group of students. The children typically have additional teachers for music, art, library/media, computer science, and physical education. Some schools also offer foreign languages. Some districts have moved sixth graders up to middle school to join seventh and eighth graders, while other school districts have found success by instructing sixth graders in their own school.

Elementary school teachers, like early education teachers, may find it rewarding to spend a whole year watching the same group of students grow and learn. They may find one year's class—with all of its individual personalities—to be entirely different from the previous year's. Elementary teachers strive to meet the academic needs of all of the children in the class, including higher- and lower-achieving students. This may mean finding

Your Future as a **TEACHER**

time to lead several reading and math groups working at different levels. The amount of time invested in encouraging children can forge a lasting bond, with many students returning to hug their favorite former teacher even after they have graduated from school.

A TYPICAL DAY: ELEMENTARY SCHOOL

Each school day is organized with time for academics, lunch, recess, snack breaks, and special classes, like art and gym. An elementary school teacher prepares ahead of time by planning what content the day's lessons will cover and coming up with related activities. This preparation also includes finding or creating books, worksheets, visual displays, and other materials for each lesson. Math and language study take up the most teaching time, especially because these two areas make up annual standardized tests.

During the course of the day, students spend time as a group learning with the teacher and spend time doing independent work. As students complete assignments, the teacher monitors their progress and helps children individually as needed. Teachers may also allow students free time in the classroom to explore learning centers or read independently. During some periods, teachers may divide the class into smaller groups based on students' skill levels in a subject. Then they lead lessons geared to the needs of each group.

The day's lessons also include some science, geography, and history, or all of these combined in some way. As an example, a class study of Native Americans can include nearly every subject and some hands-on craft

After the students go home, teachers still have plenty of work to do. They must grade papers, prepare lessons for the next day, and make sure the classroom is neat and tidy.

projects. Such a unit can reach students of all different learning styles.

As students leave the classroom for lunch or other classes, a teacher may have some time for lesson preparation, grading, or communication with parents. Or they may be scheduled to supervise children in the cafeteria or on the playground. Near the end of the school day, teachers spend time explaining homework assignments to the students. Once students are dismissed for the day, the teacher still has lots of work ahead: grading, preparing worksheets and reading materials for the next day, making

Your Future as a **TEACHER**

notes about students' behavior and progress, and cleaning up the classroom. A school may also schedule after-school meetings or professional development (extra training for teachers) with faculty and supervisors. This can make for a long day. Many teachers don't leave until 5 p.m. after arriving at school by 7:30 a.m. or earlier.

Sample Daily Schedule of an Elementary School Teacher

An elementary teacher's day is a busy one. The day is packed with activities, and there is little time to take a break from supervising students. The following is a sample schedule for a typical day:

7:15 Arrive; get coffee.

7:30 Attend early meeting. Complete any last-minute preparations.

8:00 Students arrive, unpack, and complete the "morning challenge" or "problem of the day."

8:10 Class recites the Pledge of Allegiance.

8:15 Hold a morning meeting with the class: take attendance; do lunch count; make announcements; review notes from home. Students share personal news briefly.

8:25 Teach language arts/writing lesson.

EARLY EDUCATION AND ELEMENTARY SCHOOL TEACHERS

9:00 Walk students to library, computer science, art, or physical education. Review daily tasks with teacher's assistant (if teacher has one), mark papers, and prepare for upcoming lessons.

9:40 Teach reading lesson.

10:20 Ten-minute snack/recess.

10:30 Teach math lesson.

11:15 Teach spelling lesson/lead spelling game.

11:40 Lunch/recess (may share lunch duty with another teacher); take twenty-minute break.

12:30 Students do independent reading or work at learning centers.

1:00 Teach social studies lesson.

1:40 Teach science lesson.

2:20 Explain homework. School chorus takes a few students out of class; remaining students work together as teams on a project.

2:35 Quick game, if time permits.

2:40 Have students clean up and pack up for dismissal. Dismiss students to parents, caregivers, or the bus.

3:00 Hold a parent conference (when necessary); mark papers; answer phone calls and emails; get ready for the next day's activities. Decorate bulletin boards. Straighten up desk and classroom.

By 5:00 Leave the school, bringing any unfinished work to complete at home.

Your Future as a **TEACHER**

CLASSROOM MANAGEMENT

Keeping a classroom of students focused is no small job. All the children bring their own feelings and energy levels to the group. Children may be tired, hungry, stressed, excited, restless, or even angry. They may be resisting the very idea of being in school that day.

To bring a level of focus, teachers need to create a clear structure in a classroom. In elementary school, teachers give a certain rhythm to the day. They do this by setting up a daily schedule to help the classroom run smoothly. These routines help students get involved in each learning activity and behave appropriately. Routines also help signal the beginning and end of each activity. In older grades, this structure becomes more academic in nature. For example, there may be a certain pace to projects and a certain day each week for quizzes.

Children, like adults, work best when there is a goal. As a result, many successful teachers use incentives, or rewards, to keep students focused. Kindergarten and early elementary students might be rewarded with daily stars on a chart; some teachers allow them to choose a small prize when they have a certain number of stars. Older students respond to different incentives. They might enjoy a movie at the end of a productive week or earn a pass to have a homework assignment eliminated.

A classroom's physical space also helps shape how children learn. This is especially important in the early grades. Teachers create visual displays and stations around the room that help physically and mentally organize kids. For example, an elementary school classroom often includes a large calendar. For younger children, the teacher

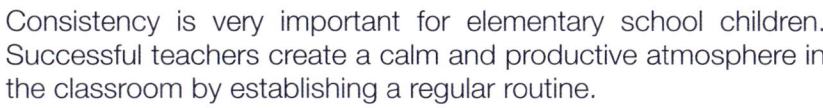

Consistency is very important for elementary school children. Successful teachers create a calm and productive atmosphere in the classroom by establishing a regular routine.

may also post the day's weather; older students might see notes telling when projects are due. Bulletin boards with student work and photographs can help the children feel that they are a meaningful part of the class. Holiday displays can guide students toward what's next, both seasonally and in their work.

CURRICULUM PLANNING

Schools expect that, by the end of the year, students in each grade will have learned certain concepts and skills.

Your Future as a TEACHER

However, it is often up to the teacher to ask, "What are the engaging ways we can get there, and how will students demonstrate that they've learned what I want them to learn?"

Children learn best when they are interested in what they are learning. Successful teachers come up with creative lesson plans that let kids explore and discover independently.

EARLY EDUCATION AND ELEMENTARY SCHOOL TEACHERS

To answer these questions, a teacher creates units of study within each subject area. For example, a teacher may create a unit on plants for earth science or a unit on multiplication for math. Each unit contains a series of lesson plans. A lesson plan is a description of a specific lesson. It explains what students will learn that day and how it will be presented to them. Teacher training programs include lesson plan development, and student teaching assignments allow lesson plans to be tested with children.

A well-developed lesson plan includes the title of the lesson, the time needed to complete it, and the materials required. It also states the lesson's objective, or what the student will do or know by the end of the lesson. Within the plan, the teacher outlines how the lesson will progress. An innovative plan brings different skills together—science and writing, for example. Depending on the teacher's goals for the lesson, the plan may center on a group activity or individual learning. Finally, the plan explains how students will be evaluated. For example, the teacher may look at student work from the lesson to determine what students have learned and what they still need to master. This part of the teaching process is called assessment.

After the lesson is completed with students, the teacher notes its successes and failures and how to improve it. Teachers who have been teaching for many years learn which lesson plans work well and which ones don't. They may keep using a lesson plan year after year if it is a lesson that proves to be particularly engaging and educational.

Your Future as a TEACHER

Depending on a school's procedures, the principal may require each teacher to submit lesson plans in advance on a regular basis, such as weekly. Other principals may be more informal and may just want to know that lesson plans are being prepared. Teachers can research and design their own lesson plans, or find all kinds of sample lesson plans online. They may also share resources with other teachers at their school or in online communities about which lesson plans are particularly successful.

Chapter 3

MIDDLE SCHOOL AND HIGH SCHOOL TEACHERS

Working with teenagers is very different from working with young children. There are pros and cons to both, but most aspiring teachers have an idea of which grade levels they'd like to work with. Teachers who want to work with middle school or high school students should consider which subject or subjects they are interested in teaching. This will enable them to better plan their careers and obtain the appropriate qualifications.

TEACHING MIDDLE SCHOOL AND HIGH SCHOOL

In middle school and high school, most teachers specialize in teaching one academic subject, such as history, English, or Spanish, to many different classes. Teachers need to complete sufficient coursework, such as a college major in the subject they teach. They must

Your Future as a TEACHER

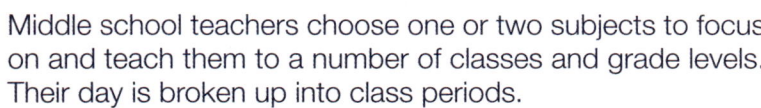

Middle school teachers choose one or two subjects to focus on and teach them to a number of classes and grade levels. Their day is broken up into class periods.

MIDDLE SCHOOL AND HIGH SCHOOL TEACHERS

also take education courses in which they learn methods for teaching the subject. Each subject teacher might also have a homeroom class, or a group of students who begin or end the day in the class, for attendance, announcements, and other guidance.

In high school, music (vocal and instrumental) and art classes are often part of a student's week. Also, students typically find many extracurricular clubs, sports teams, and performing arts groups to join after school. Teachers who are paid to lead these groups usually enjoy the chance to work with students outside the classroom and share their expertise in an area of interest.

Teachers at the middle and high school levels interact with more students for a smaller amount of time. The school day is broken up into units of instruction that might last for one or two periods. As a result, teachers need to get in and out of lessons quickly and

35

smoothly and build the subject a little each day. Concepts are explored in more depth at this level, and teachers create more tests and writing assignments to measure students' progress. Because secondary teachers are trained in their subjects, they are expected to be good sources of information.

The schedules of middle and high schools tend to build in more breaks for teachers. Some schools give teachers a prep period during the day devoted to grading, lecture preparation, and other tasks. During free periods, a teacher may also be assigned to monitor a study hall or homeroom.

Day in the Life of a Ninth-Grade Teacher

Julia G. Thompson is a ninth-grade English teacher in a large suburban high school near Washington, DC. She described a typical day at work in a profile on Monster.com.

<u>5:45 – 6:10</u> Drive to work. There is usually a lot of traffic!

<u>6:15 – 7:20</u> Arrive at work. Prepare the classroom before the students arrive. "If I need to clean the board, I hit that first and then wipe down the

MIDDLE SCHOOL AND HIGH SCHOOL TEACHERS

	desks with disinfectant. I connect the laptop, check email, and scribble everything that the kids need to know on the board."
7:20 – 9:00	The first class. "Because this is such a long period, I try to break up assignments and alternate types of activities."
9:00 – 9:15	Break.
9:15 – 10:55	The second class—"the same as the first but with a few tweaks to meet the needs of a different set of students."
11:02 – 11:28	Lunch. It's a large school so there are several lunch periods. "Sometimes I have lunch duty but it is not unpleasant, just noisy."
11:33 – 1:13	Planning period, which includes lots of time spent grading papers.
1:20 – 2:10	Last class of the day. "The kids can be tired so it is challenging to keep them upbeat and focused."
2:10 – 3:45	"I stay after school four days a week to help students make up work, get extra help on writing assignments, or just work on problems they are having with the material…. Right before I leave, I make sure the room is clean and my desk clear."

Your Future as a **TEACHER**

SPECIAL SUBJECTS AND SERVICES

A school depends on its specialized teachers to "round out" a child's education with art, music, instrumental music, physical education, and vocational classes. A specialized art teacher receives his or her training in that particular art form or skill, but also learns teaching methods and techniques.

Special subject teachers help students learn in different, but no less valuable, ways than regular classroom teachers do. Special subject teachers can play an important role in a student's education. A child who has a hard time focusing on reading may be the same child who comes to life in a music class. Another child who gets discouraged by math might be a gifted athlete in gym. As for the teachers, they often enjoy the variety that comes from working with children in many different age groups. They may also work with many of the same students from year to year.

MIDDLE SCHOOL AND HIGH SCHOOL TEACHERS

Some teachers become special subject teachers. They teach subjects such as art, music, drama, or physical education to help give students a well-rounded education.

Your Future as a **TEACHER**

Special education teachers play a unique role in a school. Special education teachers serve students with learning disabilities, physical disabilities, and other special needs. Working with children whose disabilities range from mild to severe, special education teachers bring extra training to their jobs. The students they work with may have a variety of learning issues. Students may have learning disabilities, such as dyslexia, hearing or speech disabilities, emotional disturbances, or autism, just to name a few. Teachers who work with these students use special teaching methods and techniques to help them learn. Because of the demands of this job, many states require special education teachers to have a master's degree in the field.

Teaching jobs in special education are growing at a faster rate than regular teaching jobs. This rise comes as more children are screened for disabilities earlier in life in order for them to get the help they need. Evidence has shown that children whose learning difficulties are identified and addressed early on have more success in school and later in their lives. In addition, federal laws require that students who need special services in school receive them. In many areas of the country, there is a shortage of teachers who are trained in special education. As a result, teachers with the required training are in high demand.

BRINGING STUDENTS UP TO STANDARDS

Since 2001, US federal law has required public schools to show that all students are meeting academic standards. In 2010, the Common Core State Standards Initiative was

Students in the United States take standardized tests to demonstrate that they are meeting the appropriate standards in English and math.

introduced, setting standardized guidelines for what each student in US public schools should know by the end of each grade. Schools must demonstrate that students are doing reading, writing, and math work at the appropriate grade level, as measured by state tests.

How does this affect the rhythms of the classroom? In many places, especially in urban areas, teachers are required to spend a large portion of the day on reading and math or assigning work that looks similar to the test.

As even kindergarten classes dive into academic work, some students do well with the increased test prep time, and others do not. Since so much time must be spent preparing for standardized tests, some teachers find they need to eliminate other topics, projects, and ways of learning. Some teachers worry that the creative parts of being a student are lost because schools put so much emphasis on teaching to the tests.

In addition, teachers say they feel pressure for all of their students to succeed on these tests, regardless of any learning issues students may have. School test results are now widely published online and in newspapers, and they can affect the status of schools as well as the amount of government money schools receive. As a result, the worry of administrators can trickle down to teacher supervisors and then to teachers themselves.

It's unlikely that student tests will disappear anytime soon. If anything, teachers may be judged in the future more strictly. They may need to demonstrate innovation and student achievement at the same time. The good news? High-energy, creative teachers who motivate their students with high expectations may be rewarded more than in the past. A number of school districts are starting to experiment with merit-based systems. These new programs give teachers extra pay if their students show significant progress or improvement.

ASSESSING STUDENTS AND COMMUNICATING WITH PARENTS

Teachers need to define how each child's social and academic progress will be assessed, or judged, during the school year. They can accomplish much of this through

MIDDLE SCHOOL AND HIGH SCHOOL TEACHERS

daily grading of assignments and quizzes, as well as observation and note taking. Students and their parents see the feedback teachers give when they check student work. Also, the patterns of reward that a teacher uses to manage a class can provide each student with feedback on his or her behavior. Some teachers even ask students to participate in assessment and to judge their own progress. A teacher can also use assessments to measure what the class as a whole understands and which concepts continue to be a struggle. As a result, the teacher can tweak upcoming lessons to meet students' needs.

Teachers meet with their students' parents at regular parent-teacher conferences. It's important to be able to speak honestly but tactfully about how each student is doing.

Your Future as a **TEACHER**

Parents and teachers come together for regular parent-teacher conferences during the year. At this time, the regular notes a teacher takes can help paint a larger picture of the child's growth through the school year. Teachers can also help parents understand how their child manages within the social worlds of school. If successful, these conferences are a wonderful way for parents and teachers to become partners in challenging, encouraging, and helping a child.

Teachers share their assessments in a more formal way through report cards and progress reports. Learning how to write these reports in an honest yet polite and helpful way is another important skill that teachers must develop.

SCHOOL-WIDE COOPERATION

When teachers work well together, their students benefit. All of the classes in a grade can come together for special projects or learning units, for instance. Schools have also found great success when older and younger students work together, with the older students acting as guides. Older students can read to younger children or teach them how to play chess. In some schools, older and younger students work together in outdoor cleanup projects while learning about their ecosystem. Service projects of this nature can involve every grade. The first line of cooperation for a successful project is teachers, who work together to develop an idea, plan the parts of the project, and set aside time for students to participate.

Chapter 4

GETTING YOUR FIRST TEACHING JOB

Once teachers have obtained their license to teach, they can begin thinking about what kind of a school they'd like to teach at. The experience of teaching varies a lot from one school to another, so it's a good idea to think carefully about the kind of school you'd like to work at. Going to job interviews and starting your first job as a teacher can be overwhelming, so it is helpful if you know what to expect and are well prepared.

ASKING QUESTIONS

Schools, even ones in the same town, can be very different from one another. To decide where they would like to teach, teaching candidates can ask questions of each school

Your Future as a TEACHER

When you're applying for teaching jobs or going for interviews, carefully consider whether you would enjoy working at the specific school.

GETTING YOUR FIRST TEACHING JOB

they investigate: What is the school's larger "culture" and vision of teaching? For example, some schools allow students to talk and be boisterous in the hallways, while others require children to walk in silent, orderly rows. Teachers will be happiest if their own vision is a good match with the school's.

It is also a good idea to learn more about the school community to understand the needs of the students. Are there many students who speak English as a second language? How many students are in special education programs? Has the community been growing or shrinking in size and why? How does the school perform on state standardized tests, and will these tests play a large role in the school year? What is the teacher turnover rate, or how many teachers are leaving the school each year? For those who have remained, how long have they been teaching there?

Practical questions are also important. If the job requires a move to a new area, what kind of community is it? Also, it is helpful to learn about the pay and benefits that the school offers. Is the pay good for that part of the state or country? What benefits will be provided? Would it be possible to get more training and become an administrator, curriculum coordinator, or other specialist in the future?

GETTING INTERVIEWS

Once teaching candidates have completed course requirements and applied for state licensure (or completed the requirements for alternative certification), they are ready to begin interviewing for positions. School districts looking to collect résumés will advertise online, but this means the district could be flooded with hundreds of résumés. After narrowing down their search, candidates can beat the crowd by researching and writing to schools directly and expressing interest in working there. They can even call or email to ask about available positions. The district staff may know of a position that is about to open up, giving an eager job hunter a spot at the head of the line. These activities will take some time but may speed up the job search in the long run. It is also a more active approach than simply waiting along with all the other candidates who responded to an ad.

Job seekers can also ask any working teachers they know if their school has any teachers scheduled for retirement soon. After sending a résumé and cover letter to the school district's human resources department, people can also forward copies to the school principal. This increases the chances of securing an interview.

GETTING YOUR FIRST TEACHING JOB

What to Expect in Your Job Interview

Interviews are always nerve-racking, but if you are prepared with responses to some commonly asked questions, you are likely to feel much less nervous. In a 2014 article in the *Guardian*, some principals—sometimes known as headteachers in the United Kingdom—shared their favorite questions to ask potential teachers during job interviews.

(continued on the next page)

When you get a job interview for a teaching position, spend some time thinking about the kinds of questions you might be asked. Be prepared to talk about why you are passionate about teaching.

Your Future as a TEACHER

(continued from the previous page)

If I walked into your classroom during an outstanding lesson, what would I see and hear? "After hearing a candidate's response, I try to get them to talk about their experiences in the classroom. I try to get a sense of the impact that they have had on pupils' achievement."—Helen Anthony, headteacher, Fortisimere School

Why do we teach x in schools? "This question really throws people. If it is math or English they sometimes look back at you as if you are mad. They assume it is obvious—a very dangerous assumption—and then completely fail to justify the subject's existence."—John Kendall, headteacher, Risca Community Comprehensive School

If you overheard some colleagues talking about you, what would they say? "This is one of my favorite questions because it gets candidates to think about their contribution to the school organization and their team spirit."—Tim Browse, headteacher, Hillcrest Primary School

If a job hunter wants to expand a search, he or she may be eligible to teach in a neighboring state, thanks to reciprocity agreements that states offer to those with certification elsewhere. Each state's reciprocity agreements are different, so it is important to check.

College career counselors have a wealth of information for teachers. They may have information on upcoming teacher job fairs. At a job fair, aspiring teachers can have a mini-interview with a school representative and then follow

GETTING YOUR FIRST TEACHING JOB

up on available positions. The college employment office may also know of state or county programs that help get new teachers into the classrooms where they are needed.

If the school district where you want to work has no job openings, you may decide to apply to work as a teacher's aide or substitute teacher in that school district. Being present in the school can help with a job search because principals prefer to hire someone who is already a tested asset to the school.

PRESENTING: THE NEW TEACHER

When attending a job fair, meeting school administrators, or interviewing for a teaching position, it is important to already look the part of a teacher. Your best bet is to dress neatly and conservatively. Learning about the school ahead of time shows that candidates are serious about their career and would be a good addition to the staff. At job fairs, job hunters have only about thirty seconds to make an impression, unless the discussion turns into a sit-down interview. Either way, candidates can practice how to "sell" themselves—or sum up unique strengths—so they can share that information clearly and directly when the chance comes.

THE BEGINNING TEACHER

All new jobs have a learning curve, but new teachers stand in front of a class on day one and are asked to do the same job as experienced veterans. Instead of having the chance to ease into the profession, beginning teachers are often given the most difficult jobs or classes.

Your Future as a TEACHER

A career as a teacher has a fast learning curve. It can be intimidating to stand in front of a class of kids for the first time, but new teachers must be prepared to dive right in.

GETTING YOUR FIRST TEACHING JOB

New teachers are most in need at schools where more teachers have left, sometimes because of the challenges there. Also, new teachers must learn to teach their own classes and navigate relationships with parents, administrators, and other teachers at the same time.

How do beginning teachers increase their chances of success? Participating in a mentoring program can make a big difference. A mentoring program provides new teachers with a more experienced "coach" who teaches at a similar grade level. In such a program, new teachers can find an outlet for questions, concerns, and frustrations. The mentor can share general wisdom or suggest practical solutions to classroom challenges. Stephanie Hansen, a Chicago kindergarten teacher, told *Catalyst Chicago* magazine that her mentor helped her find an alternative to helping twenty-three students at once. "I was walking around trying to see what [one] student had written, while keeping [other students] focused on the assignment. And they all wanted my attention." Her mentor suggested she break the class into small groups that met daily, allowing her to spend time with each child in the group. It worked. "It is a much more organized workshop, and my students' writing has improved," she reported.

An experienced teacher can help put things in perspective. It can be hard for new teachers to not take things personally, such as an insult from a student. The first few years as a teacher often require strength and endurance. A mentor can keep a new teacher focused on his or her success stories instead of the problems. As studies show how important they are, more and more schools are creating mentoring programs. Even if a school does not offer a formal mentoring program, a new teacher can still request to have a mentor.

ADVANCING IN YOUR CAREER

There are many opportunities for advancement for experienced teachers. Experienced teachers may become lead teachers or mentors. In these roles, they help newer teachers to work on their teaching skills. Teachers may decide they want to obtain additional certification to become a school counselor or school librarian. Others may go on to become an instructional coordinator, who oversees the school's curriculum and teaching standards. This involves developing class materials and coordinating with teachers and principals to evaluate their effectiveness.

There is also the option to become a principal or assistant principal. These positions require additional training. Principals must have a master's degree in

One of the strongest forms of support for teachers is other teachers. Don't be afraid to ask your coworkers for advice. They will probably be happy to offer their insight.

educational administration or leadership, and they need to have experience working as a teacher.

Some teachers aren't interested in advancing to any of these positions. Often, the reason that people pursue a career in teaching is because they want to teach children. As many of the advanced positions in schools don't involve teaching, many teachers prefer to stay in the classroom and continue working directly with children.

Chapter 5

THE FUTURE OF TEACHING

The employment growth rate of public school teachers depends upon state and local funding. According to the Bureau of Labor Statistics 2018 data, demand for teachers was projected to rise by 8 percent between 2016 and 2026, which is the average rate for all occupations. This growth will be due to rising student enrollment. However, this figure varies from state to state and from school to school. Teachers who specialize in subjects that are particularly in demand, and who have some flexibility in terms of job location, will have better chances of finding jobs. There may also be an increased demand for early childhood teachers, due to the trend toward making pre-kindergarten programs more widely available.

THE FUTURE OF TEACHING

WHERE WILL THE TEACHING JOBS BE?

There are usually more available teaching positions in urban or rural communities than in suburban ones. Inner-city public schools have a harder time keeping new teachers and usually have openings each year. Urban schools especially need teachers with energy and imagination, as they often include students from low-income backgrounds or who have recently emigrated from other countries. In addition, as more English as a second language (ESL)

There is a strong demand for teachers who are trained to work with ESL learners. If you are bilingual or can teach in both English and Spanish, your job prospects are good.

57

students enter US schools, schools need teachers who are trained to work with these populations or bilingual teachers who can teach in both English and Spanish.

In 2009, the Boston Plan for Excellence in the Public Schools found that new city teachers needed help and coaching from experienced teachers to have a good first year. Since then, Boston schools have tried to pair new teachers with a mentor. Other cities may or may not have this type of program. Those interested in working at an urban school should find out how they support their new teachers through the first few years of teaching.

In rural areas, towns have fewer residents and fewer students in school. Usually, fewer people compete for the available teaching jobs since many of the area's young adults may have moved away. Rural schools usually pay lower salaries than suburban and urban areas, especially if the area has a lower cost of living. However, for those who can move to a rural town to teach and would enjoy country life, this can be a good choice.

CHARTER AND PRIVATE SCHOOLS

Students and their families may have choices about their children's education, especially in areas where the public schools are not strong. Charter schools and private schools provide an alternative to public schools.

A charter school is an experimental public school that is granted a charter by its state to operate independently. Charter schools are given state money to operate, but they do not have to follow the same rules as the other public schools in the area. They have the freedom to establish their own missions, goals, and approaches to education.

Charter schools are publicly funded, but they do not have to follow the same rules and curriculum as public schools. They often have a specific educational philosophy.

They are smaller, enrolling about half the students of the average public school. Most charter schools have a clear approach to teaching and look for teachers who will follow it. For example, a charter school's approach might include strict behavioral and academic discipline or an environmentally based study of all subjects. In order to keep its charter, each charter school must show the same strong grades and test scores as public schools.

Interest in charter schools has grown, and many people, especially in urban communities, are pleased that their children have this option. However, the success

Your Future as a TEACHER

rates of charter schools are mixed, and charter schools that show low test scores or another kind of failure can be closed by the state. Charter schools may grow slowly since states can cap the size of these schools. Moreover, these schools receive less state money than public schools. In 2018, seven states did not allow charter schools at all.

Private schools enroll students whose families pay tuition. While teachers in training who want to work at a private school might imagine themselves working on a large, beautiful campus with stone buildings, most private schools are smaller and found in urban areas. They may be religious in orientation—most often Catholic—and may include religious lessons as part of the students' education. Private school teachers find they have more say over how they would like to run their classroom and what they would like to teach. However, these schools do expect that teachers will support the institution's religious goals. Many private schools are able to choose the students they accept, and so the students may be strong learners.

Overall, the number of students in all grades at private schools has grown smaller since 1990. Because they run on tuition money and donations, private schools can be hit harder by recessions, and private school teachers do not usually have the protection of tenure. Also, private schools typically offer smaller salaries than public schools and may not have the same retirement and health benefits. With smaller staffs, they also may ask teachers to be more involved in extracurricular clubs and teams.

Positive Discipline in the Classroom

Many new teachers struggle with maintaining control in the classroom and managing students with a range of personality types. Dr. Jane Nelson, the author of *Positive Discipline in the Classroom*, provides advice on how to handle various disciplinary issues on her website, PositiveDiscipline.com. In response to one teacher's question about how to handle constant classroom chatter, Dr. Nelson had the following suggestion:

"My favorite suggestion for all classroom problems is to use class meetings to let the kids find solutions. They are good at it. They are motivated to follow suggestions they help create, and they learn problem-solving skills."

Every classroom has at least one child who is a "yakker." Nelson says, "whether teachers see the yakker as enjoyable, irritating, or rude, it does not eliminate the fact that the 'gift of gab' is a talent. Teachers can value this talent while guiding students with the 'gift of gab' to use their talent in ways that enhance the learning in the classroom."

One way to do this is to give the yakker a verbal job, such as introducing new students or making announcements. Other positive disciplinary responses include setting up a signal response to indicate to the student that he or she is talking too much, waiting and watching before explaining to a student that he or she is being disruptive, and having an honest conversation with the student, for example, "I feel frustrated when I repeat directions several times and I wish that I only had to give them once."

However, there are also advantages to teaching at a private school. Some private schools offer teachers discounted housing on the campus. Private schools may also give a new teacher more freedom in the classroom, including more choice in what and how to teach. This can be nice for those who would like to experiment with different approaches and see what works best with their students.

THE LURE OF SUMMERS OFF

When discussing a career as a teacher, many people cite the perk of summers off. Most teachers in the United States receive the traditional two-month break after a ten-month school year. While some people consider such a schedule to be a luxury, many teachers believe it is a necessity to take a break from the intensity of school. Philadelphia-area teacher Anna Weiss, writing for the *Philadelphia Public School Notebook*, points out that the summer break may be the only way some teachers avoid career burnout. "I personally work about sixty to seventy hours a week," she says. "It's more than I'm contracted to work, but I willingly do it because in teaching, it's just a given that you're going to work outside of the school day."

Teachers use the time off in different ways. For example, many teachers work a second job to bring in additional income. While some decide to exercise completely different skills during the summertime, others directly apply their teaching skills to positions as tutors, summer-session instructors, or camp staffers. Many teachers use the time off to do professional development, attending summer

Teachers work very hard year round, and they are rewarded with long summer breaks. Some teachers get summer jobs to earn extra income, while others enjoy time with their families.

courses or conferences that will help them improve their teaching. Instead of working or studying, other teachers may travel or spend time with their families.

However, the traditional teaching schedule may be changing. Some schools have shifted to (or will shift to) a year-round schedule with regular breaks. The year-round schedule varies from school to school. In one model, students attend school for forty-five days and then have a break for fifteen days. In another model, students go to school for sixty days and then have a break for twenty days.

This new schedule is more common in urban areas. Educators have found that the constant structure prevents summer learning loss and removes some of the risks to children that an unstructured summer might bring. According to a 2018 article by Grace Chen in *Public School Review*, nearly 4 percent of children in the United States attend year-round school. This number is rising as increasing numbers of education experts weigh in on the benefits of the year-round calendar. In an article in *Educational Leadership* journal, Tracy A. Huebner writes, "Research indicates that summer learning loss is a real problem for students—especially for economically disadvantaged students. In one study, Alexander, Entwisle, and Olson (2007) found that low-income students made similar achievement gains to other students during the school year; the widening of the achievement gap between the two groups occurred over the summer."

THE FUTURE CLASSROOM

What skills will be needed for the classroom of the future? Technology will play a large role. Many teachers already post homework assignments and student grades with online tools. Most schools have replaced chalkboards with whiteboards, which can be used for both traditional lessons and computer-based lessons. The entire classroom is becoming more "virtual," with lessons posted online and assignments typed up and posted instead of handed in on paper. As students continue to turn to the internet for research and study help, school libraries are expanding these services. Students are increasingly accessing the information they need through e-books and online

Technology is becoming more and more common in classrooms across the country, even for the youngest learners. Technology can be helpful in some ways but distracting in others.

databases. According to a 2017 article in *Edudemic*, three out of four educators use some sort of technology in their classroom every day. Small laptops and tablets, especially Chromebooks, are among the most popular devices used in classrooms because they are lightweight and easy to use.

Some teachers find that technology helps them reach students who learn differently. Visual and auditory learners, for instance, seem to learn best when they can see and hear a lesson with multiple forms of media. Tactile (hands-on) learners may learn best when they can get out of

Your Future as a TEACHER

their chairs and do a presentation or experiment. Using technology to serve different kinds of learners will probably become more common in the future.

Not all teachers are fans of the rise of technology in the classroom. Some feel that too much access to technology leads to students wasting time on social media. Also, many schools cannot afford to invest in the latest devices. However, teachers who understand how to use technology (or who are willing to be trained) will have an edge in the job market, especially at schools that are eager to try new things and involve students in new ways.

It is an exciting time to be a teacher. Schools are looking for new ideas and want to challenge students in new ways. Learning is becoming more hands-on and interactive to better serve students who are hungry to understand the world around them. Teachers have a direct impact on the next generation. Their work is an investment that is not wasted. Every successful adult has at least one story about an influential teacher. If teaching is your calling, that teacher could be you.

Glossary

ASSESSMENT The act of making a judgment about something.

AUTISM A developmental disorder that makes it hard for a person to form normal social relationships and communicate with others.

CHARTER SCHOOL An independent school that receives government funding but does not have to follow the same rules and curriculum as the other public schools in the area.

CURRICULUM The courses of study offered by a school or institution.

DYSLEXIA A learning disability that makes it hard for a person to read, write, and spell.

EARLY CHILDHOOD EDUCATION Educational programming for children who are younger than elementary school age.

ECOSYSTEM A community made up of living things such as plants, animals, and organisms as well as nonliving things such as air, water, and soil.

EVALUATE To decide on the value of something by carefully studying it.

EXTRACURRICULAR Activities that are not part of the regular curriculum.

INCENTIVE A reason to want to do something.

MOTOR SKILLS Actions that involves using muscles.

PHONICS A method of teaching reading and writing that involves connecting letters or groups of letters with sounds.

PORTFOLIO A selection of a person's work, compiled over a period of time.

Your Future as a TEACHER

PRIVATE SCHOOL A school that operates independently and is usually funded by charging tuition fees; also called an independent school.

PUBLIC SCHOOL A school that is publicly funded and free to attend. Public schools are operated by the government and required to offer a specific curriculum.

STANDARDIZED TEST A test that is given and scored in a consistent way.

TENURE A permanent job with protection from being fired.

UNION An organization of workers in a particular industry, formed to protect their rights and interests.

VETERAN TEACHER A teacher with a lot of experience in a profession.

VOCATIONAL Relating to a specific career or profession.

For More Information

American Federation of Teachers, AFL-CIO (AFT)
555 New Jersey Avenue NW
Washington, DC 20001
(202) 879-4400
Website: https://www.aft.org
Facebook and Twitter: @AFTunion
The AFT is a teacher's labor union representing 1.7 million members across the United States. It provides advocacy to protect the rights and interests of teachers.

Bureau of Labor Statistics
Postal Square Building
2 Massachusetts Avenue NE
Washington, DC 20212
(202) 691-5200
Website: https://www.bls.gov/home.htm
Twitter: @BLS_gov
The Bureau of Labor Statistics provides comprehensive information and statistics about all types of labor, including qualifications required for each profession and links to additional job information resources.

Canadian Teachers' Federation (CTF)
2490 Don Reid Drive
Ottawa, ON K1H 1E1
Canada
(613) 232-1505
Website: https://www.ctf-fce.ca/en/Pages/default.aspx
Facebook: @CTF.FCE
Twitter: @CanTeachersFed

Your Future as a TEACHER

CTF is a nonprofit membership organization providing advocacy, education, research, and events for teachers across Canada.

Council for the Accreditation of Educator Preparation (CAEP)
1140 19th Street NW, Suite 400
Washington, DC 20036
(202) 223-0077
Website: http://www.ncate.org
Twitter: @caepupdates
CAEP sets and maintains standards in teaching by providing accreditation for education providers across the United States.

National Board for Professional Teaching Standards (NBPTS)
1525 Wilson Boulevard, Suite 700
Arlington, VA 22209
(703) 465-2700
Website: https://www.nbpts.org
Facebook: @TheNBPTS
Twitter: @NBPTS
NBPTS provides professional certification for teachers across the United States.

National Council for Teachers of English (NCTE)
1111 West Kenyon Road
Urbana, IL 61801
(217) 328-3870
Website: http://www2.ncte.org

FOR MORE INFORMATION

Facebook and Twitter: @NCTE.org
NCTE is a membership organization for teachers of English and language arts. It provides professional support through publications, meetings, and online resources such as lesson plans.

National Education Association (NEA)
1201 16th Street NW
Washington, DC 20036
(202) 833-4000
Website: http://www.nea.org
Facebook and Twitter: @NEAtoday
NEA is a labor union for teachers. It provides advocacy and education for teachers across the United States.

TEACH.org
Website: https://www.teach.org
Facebook and Instagram: @teach.org
Twitter: @TEACHorg
TEACH.org is a nonprofit organization launched by the US Department of Education and Microsoft. It provides training and career resources for aspiring teachers across the United States.

Teach for Canada
215 Spadina Avenue, Suite 550
Toronto, ON M5T 2C7
Canada
(647) 886-0640
Website: https://teachforcanada.ca/en
Facebook, Instagram, and Twitter: @teachforcanada

Your Future as a **TEACHER**

Teach for Canada is a nonprofit organization that works to recruit and support northern First Nations teachers, with the goal of making education more equal.

To Become a Teacher
Website: http://tobecomeateacher.org
Facebook: @ToBecomeATeacherOrg
Twitter: @2becomeateacher
To Become a Teacher is a website providing comprehensive career information for teachers in the United States, including information about schools, licensing, and job postings by state.

For Further Reading

Burgess, Dave. *Teach Like a Pirate: Increase Student Engagement, Boost Your Creativity, and Transform Your Life as an Educator.* San Diego, CA: Dave Burgess Consulting, Inc, 2012.

Carlson, John S., and Richard L. Carlson. *101 Careers in Education.* New York, NY: Springer Publishing Company, LLC: 2016.

Chickie-Wolfe, Louise A. *Lucky to Be a Teacher: Life-Changing Affirmations for Positive Classrooms.* New York, NY: Skyhorse Publishing, Inc., 2018.

Institute for Career Research. *Career as a Teacher: Early Childhood Education.* Chicago, IL: Institute for Career Research, 2012.

Institute for Career Research. *Career as a Teacher: Special Education.* Chicago, IL: Institute for Career Research, 2015.

La Bella, Laura. *Getting a Job in Education.* New York, NY: Rosen Publishing, 2017.

Nelson, Jane. *Positive Discipline in the Classroom.* New York, NY: Three Rivers Press, 2013.

Rogers, Brian. *Career as a Teacher: What They Do, How to Become One, and What the Future Holds!* KidLit-O Books, 2013.

Sanna, Ellyn. *Special Education Teacher.* Philadelphia, PA: Mason Crest, 2014.

Sunseri, Sophia. *Working as a Teacher in Your Community.* New York, NY: Rosen Publishing, 2016.

Bibliography

Bureau of Labor Statistics. "High School Teachers." Retrieved November 1, 2018. https://www.bls.gov/ooh/education-training-and-library/high-school-teachers.htm.

Bureau of Labor Statistics. "Kindergarten and Elementary School Teachers." Retrieved November 1, 2018. https://www.bls.gov/ooh/education-training-and-library/kindergarten-and-elementary-school-teachers.htm.

Bureau of Labor Statistics. "Middle School Teachers." Retrieved November 1, 2018. https://www.bls.gov/ooh/education-training-and-library/middle-school-teachers.htm.

C., Victoria. "A Day in the Life of a Teacher." Experience.com, June 29, 2017. https://www.experience.com/advice/careers/professions/a-day-in-the-life-of-a-teacher.

Chen, Grace. "Year Round vs. Traditional Schedule Public Schools." *Public School Review*, April 6, 2018. https://www.publicschoolreview.com/blog/year-round-vs-traditional-schedule-public-schools.

Ericksen, Kristina. "Why Become a Teacher? Educators Share What They Love About Their Work." Rasmussen College, April 13, 2015. https://www.rasmussen.edu/degrees/education/blog/why-become-a-teacher.

Huebner, Tracy A. "What Research Says About… / Year-Round Schooling." *Educational Leadership* 67, no. 7 (April 2010). http://www.ascd.org/publications/educational_leadership/apr10/vol67/num07/Year-Round_Schooling.aspx.

BIBLIOGRAPHY

Jones, George. "Classroom Technology: What's New for 2017?" *Edudemic*, January 16, 2017. http://www.edudemic.com/classroom-technology-in-2017.

Nelson, Jane. "Trouble Controlling Chatter in Classroom." *Positive Discipline*. Retrieved November 1, 2018. https://www.positivediscipline.com/articles/trouble-controlling-chatter-classroom.

Owen, Laura. "A Day in the Life of a Third Grade Teacher." Teaching.Monster.com. Retrieved November 1, 2018. http://teaching.monster.com/education/articles/8013-a-day-in-the-life-of-a-third-grade-teacher.

Ratcliffe, Rebecca. "Top 10 Questions Teachers Are Asked at Job Interviews." *The Guardian* Teacher's Blog, January 29, 2014. https://www.theguardian.com/teacher-network/teacher-blog/2014/jan/29/teacher-job-interview-questions-top-ten.

Sharp, Phil. "2017 Technology in the Classroom Survey Results." Freckle.com, November 16, 2016. http://blog.freckle.com/2016/11/17/2017-technology-in-the-classroom-survey-results#comments.

Thompson, Julia G. "A Day in the Life of a High School English Teacher." Teaching.Monster.com. Retrieved November 1, 2018. http://teaching.monster.com/careers/articles/8082-a-day-in-the-life-of-a-high-school-english-teacher.

Vilorio, Dennis. "Teaching for a Living." Bureau of Labor Statistics, June 2016. https://www.bls.gov/careeroutlook/2016/article/education-jobs-teaching-for-a-living.htm.

Weiss, Anna. "Summer Break Not Really a Break for Teachers." *Philadelphia Public School Notebook*, August 25, 2009. https://thenotebook.org/articles/2009/08/25/summer-break-not-really-a-break-for-teachers.

Williams, Debra. "Coaches Keep Rookie Teachers on Track." *Catalyst Chicago*, April 22, 2008. https://www.chicagoreporter.com/coaches-keep-rookie-teachers-track.

Wixom, Micah Ann. "50-State Comparison: Charter School Policies." Education Commission of the States, January 23, 2018. https://www.ecs.org/charter-school-policies.

Index

A
administrator, 7, 18, 42, 48, 51, 53
assessment, 31, 42–44
assistant principal, 54–55

C
certification, 10–13, 15–18, 48, 50, 54
charter school, 6, 18, 58–60
Common Core Standards, 40–42
counselor, 50, 54

D
discipline, 59, 61

E
early childhood education, 8, 9, 12, 20–23
elementary school, 6, 9, 11–12, 19, 20–24, 26–31
  classroom management, 23, 28–29, 61
  curriculum planning, 29–32
  sample daily schedule, 26–27
  typical day duties, 24–26
English as a second language (ESL), 47, 57–58
evaluation, 11, 31, 54
extracurricular activity, 35, 60

H
Hansen, Stephanie, 53–54
high school, 6, 10, 13, 15–16, 19
  academic standards, 40–42
  school-wide cooperation, 44
  student assessment, and parents, 42–44
  teaching specific subjects, 20, 33, 35–36, 38, 40
  typical daily schedule, 36–37

J
job
  career advancement, 54–55
  fair, 50–51

first teaching position, 45, 47–48, 51, 53–54
growth, 19, 56–60, 62–66
interview, 45, 47–51
stability, 8, 18–19

K

Kato, Jeaninne Escallier, 7–8

L

library, 23, 54, 64–65
license, 10–13, 15–17, 45, 48
low-income student, 57, 64

M

mentoring program, 53–54, 58
middle school, 6, 9–10, 23
  academic standards, 40–42
  school-wide cooperation, 44
  student assessment, and parents, 42–44
  teaching specific subjects, 33, 35–36, 38, 40

P

parents, and
  communication, 11, 22, 25, 27, 42–44, 53
preschool, and
  kindergarten, 6, 11, 15, 18–19, 20–23, 42, 53, 56
  classroom management, 15, 28–29
  curriculum planning, 29–32
principal, 32, 48–49, 51, 54–55
private school, 6, 11, 18–19, 58–60, 62
provisional license, 15–16
public school, 6, 10–11, 18–19, 40–41, 56–64

R

rural school, 8, 58

S

school
  board, 18, 23
  budget, 18
  district, 18, 22–23, 42, 48, 51
special education, 8, 40, 47

INDEX

special subjects, 6, 11–12, 15–16, 33–36, 38, 40, 50, 56
standardized test, 12, 24, 42, 47
suburban school, 19, 36, 57–58
supervisor, 26, 42

T

teacher
  education program, 12–13
  experience, or veteran, 16, 19, 51, 53–55, 58
  grading duties, 14, 25–26, 36–37, 43
  lesson plan, and preparation, 13–14, 24–26, 29–32, 35–36
  supervision, 11–12, 25–26
  training, 11, 16, 26, 31, 38, 40, 48, 54–55
teaching, 6–8, 15, 58
  alternate route programs, 16–18
  career advancement, 54–55
  certification, 10–13, 15–18, 48, 50, 54
  curriculum, 22, 29–32, 48, 54
  discipline, 59, 61
  first position, 45, 47–48, 51, 53–54
  internship, 13
  license, 10–13, 15–17, 45, 48
  options in, 9–11
  personality, 7–8, 10
  qualities needed in, 8, 9, 14–15
  skills, 11, 13, 54, 62, 64
  standards, 16, 54
  summer break, 62–64
  technology, 64–66
  tenure, 18, 60
Thompson, Julia G., 36–37
tutor, 62

U

union, 18–19
universal pre-K, 23
urban school, 8, 18–19, 41, 57–60, 64

V

virtual classroom, 64–65
vocational school, 18, 38

ABOUT THE AUTHORS

Rachel Given-Wilson has written and edited a number of nonfiction books for teenagers, including the Tech Girls series of books about careers for girls in STEM industries. She lives in Brooklyn with her family.

Annalise Silivanch teaches college students as area chair for the Department of Humanities at the University of Phoenix in Jersey City, New Jersey. Her college instruction experience includes coaching students to set personal and professional goals for themselves.

PHOTO CREDITS

Cover, p. 63 wavebreakmedia/Shutterstock.com; back cover, pp. 7, interior pages (background) sebra/Shutterstock.com; pp. 7 (inset), 30, 52–53, 55 Rawpixel.com/Shutterstock.com; pp. 10, 46–47 James R. Martin/Shutterstock.com; p. 12 LightField Studios/Shutterstock.com; pp. 14, 34–35, 38–39, 65 Monkey Business Images/Shutterstock.com; p. 17 fizkes/Shutterstock.com; p. 21 Sergey Zaykov/Shutterstock.com; p. 25 BarahaveStudio/Shutterstock.com; p. 29 Wolfgang Kaehler/LightRocket/Getty Images; p. 41 Kaplan Test Prep/Shutterstock.com; p. 43 Ariel Skelley/DigitalVision/Getty Images; p. 49 Phovoir/Shutterstock.com; p. 57 Gideon Mendel/Corbis Documentary/Getty Images; p. 59 Joe Raedle/Getty Images.

Design and Layout: Nicole Russo-Duca; Photo Researcher: Nicole Reinholdt